TIGER SHARK

BY ROBIN TWIDDY

BookLife
PUBLISHING

©2019
BookLife Publishing
King's Lynn
Norfolk PE30 4LS

A catalogue record for this book is available from the British Library.

ISBN: 978-1-78637-614-5

Written by:
Robin Twiddy

Edited by:
Holly Duhig

Designed by:
Danielle Rippengill

IMAGE CREDITS

All images are courtesy of Shutterstock.com, unless otherwise specified. With thanks to Getty Images, Thinkstock Photo and iStockphoto. Cover – wildestanimal, Song Heming, pirke, arka38. Boarder used throughout – arka38. Background Images – Ivan Kurmyshov, Andrey_Kuzmin, Song Heming, pirke, vovan. 2 – HQuality. 4 – Shane Gross. 5 – Fiona Ayerst. 6 – Matthew R McClure. 7 – Matt9122. 8 – A Cotton Photo. 9 – VisionDive. 10 – le bouil baptiste. 11 – Matt9122. 12 – wildestanimal. 13 – Greg Amptman. 14 – HQuality. 15 – A Cotton Photo. 16 – Greg Amptman, Marc Henauer. 17 – Michael Bogner. 18 – Michael Bogner. 19 – Yoshinori. 20 – VisionDive, Petr Jilek, Ondrej Prosicky, Shane Myers Photography. 21 – Alexandra Childs. 22 – le bouil baptiste. 23 – frantisekhojdysz.

CONTENTS

WORDS THAT LOOK LIKE <u>this</u> CAN BE FOUND IN THE GLOSSARY ON PAGE 24.

THE TIGER SHARK

There are around 440 known species of shark. Some are small, and some are large. Sharks have **evolved** for millions of years to be the **apex predators** of the ocean.

BITING FACTS:
THE TIGER SHARK'S SCIENTIFIC NAME IS GALEOCERDO CUVIER.

The tiger shark is the fourth-largest shark after the whale shark, the basking shark and the great white shark.

BITING FACTS:
TIGER SHARKS USUALLY LIVE AND HUNT ALONE, EXCEPT DURING THE MATING SEASON.

Male tiger sharks can grow to between 3.25 and 4.25 metres (m) long, but the female tends to grow to around 5 m! They are mostly found in open **tropical** waters.

TEETH

The tiger shark has roughly 48 teeth in total, with 24 on the top jaw and 24 on the lower jaw.

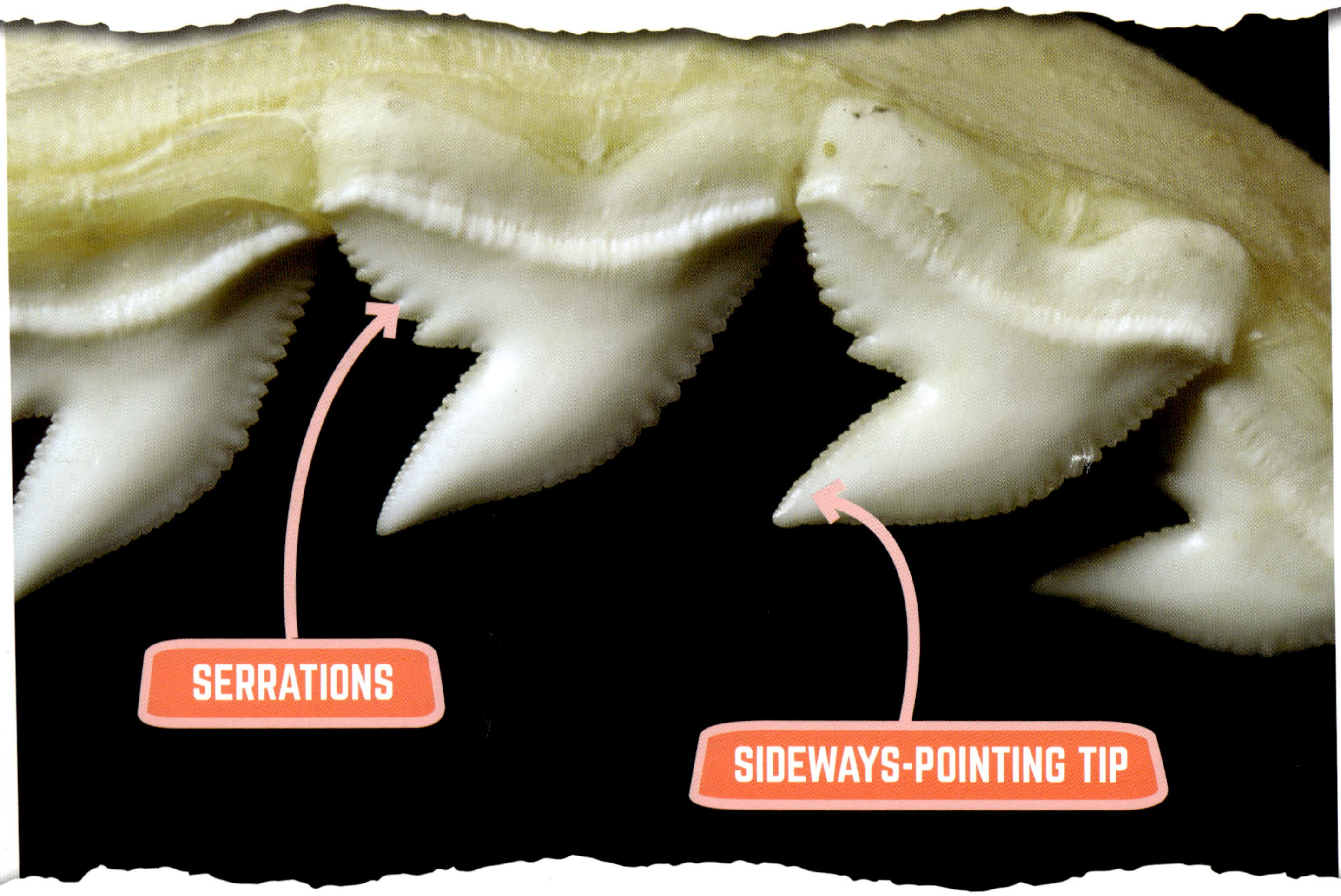

The tiger shark's teeth are very **unique**. They are very sharp with large **serrations** and tips that point sideways towards the edge of the mouth.

BITING FACTS:
TIGER SHARKS EAT THE WIDEST RANGE OF PREY OF ALL SHARKS.

The tiger shark's hooked and serrated teeth give it one of the most dangerous bites of all sharks. These teeth can cut through flesh, bone and even turtle shells!

NOSE

Like other sharks, the tiger shark has an excellent sense of smell.

This helps it to hunt its prey. The tiger shark doesn't breathe through its nostrils – called nares – but only uses them to smell.

The tiger shark has a wedge-shaped head. This means that it has a nose that is much wider and flatter than most other sharks'. This wedge shape helps them to turn tightly on the spot.

SKELETON

Shark skeletons are not made of bone like land animals' skeletons. Their skeletons are made of **cartilage**. It is lighter and more flexible than bone, allowing the shark to float more easily.

BITING FACTS:
TIGER SHARKS ARE NOT PICKY EATERS. THEY HAVE EVEN BEEN KNOWN TO EAT TYRES AND NUMBER PLATES!

Cartilage breaks down much quicker than bone, so it is rare to find a complete shark skeleton.

Cartilage is flexible; this means that sharks can turn in the water farther and faster than animals with skeletons made of bone.

EYES

The tiger shark has excellent eyesight. These sharks are nocturnal, which means they sleep in the day and hunt at night. Their eyes are very good at seeing in dark or murky water.

BITING FACTS:
THE TIGER SHARK HAS A SPIRACLE (SAY: SPI-RA-CALL) BEHIND ITS EYES. THIS IS A SPECIAL GILL FOR TAKING IN OXYGEN.

BITING FACTS:
IN NATIVE HAWAIIAN MYTHOLOGY THE TIGER SHARK'S EYES CAN GIVE SOMEONE THE ABILITY TO SEE THE FUTURE!

When the tiger shark attacks its prey, it can pull a special see-through eyelid over its eye to protect it. This is called a nictitating (say: nict-i-tate-ing) membrane.

FINS

All sharks have either four or five types of fin. The tiger shark has five types of fin. These are:

Each fin has a different job. Some keep the shark upright in the water. Others help it to swim. The tiger shark can be recognised by how close its second dorsal fin is to its tail.

SKIN

Shark skin is covered in tiny, tooth-like scales, called dermal denticles. These are made from the same material as their teeth, which makes their skin tough, like armour.

The tiger shark is named after its distinctive markings which are similar to a tiger's. These stripes fade as the shark grows.

Its dorsal side (the top of the shark) ranges from blue to light green and its underside is either a yellow or white colour.

TAIL

The tail fin is called the caudal fin. This is the fin that the shark uses to speed up and slow down. The tiger shark's caudal fin is longer on the top than the bottom.

BITING FACTS:
THE TIGER SHARK MOVES AT AN AVERAGE SPEED OF FOUR TO FIVE KILOMETRES AN HOUR (KPH), BUT CAN MOVE AT SHORT BURSTS OF UP TO 32 KPH.

The tiger shark is one of the strongest swimmers of all the grey sharks, but it tends to swim slowly. The shape of its caudal fin allows it to move in a quick burst when it gets close to its prey.

FOOD CHAIN

Food chains show us which animals eat each other. The tiger shark is well known for its appetite. It will try to eat most things that come across its path, including smaller sharks.

The tiger shark will eat smaller fish (including smaller sharks), dolphins, seals, **crustaceans** and sea turtles.

Tiger sharks have been found with all sorts of animals inside their stomachs, including dogs, porpoises, and even a horse's head.

BITING FACTS:
TIGER SHARKS ARE ALSO SCAVENGERS, WHICH MEANS THEY SOMETIMES EAT ANIMALS THAT ARE ALREADY DEAD.

LIFE CYCLE

The tiger shark is ovoviviparous (say: oh-vo-vi-vi-par-us).

BITING FACTS:
IT'S BELIEVED THAT TIGER SHARKS LIVE TO AROUND 27 YEARS OLD.

This means that the babies grow inside an egg, but then hatch after around 11 months, whilst still inside the mother.

The tiger shark can have a litter of between 10 and 80 baby sharks, called pups.

BITING FACTS:
AFTER THEY HATCH, THE BABIES STAY INSIDE THE MOTHER FOR AROUND FOUR TO FIVE MONTHS.

A baby tiger shark measures around 51 to 76 centimetres long. The tiger shark pups leave their mothers after birth to fend for themselves.

GLOSSARY

APEX PREDATORS	animals that are at the top of the food chain and are not prey for another animal
CAMOUFLAGE	traits that allow an animal to hide itself in a habitat
CARTILAGE	a flexible tissue that acts like bone in some fish such as sharks
CRUSTACEANS	a type of animal that lives in water and has a hard outer shell
EVOLVED	developed over a long time to become adapted to a certain habitat
GILL	the organ that some animals use to breathe underwater
MATING SEASON	a particular time when a species of animal mates to produce young
MYTHOLOGY	the stories and legends of a culture that often explain their history or environment
OXYGEN	a natural gas that all living things need in order to survive
PREY	animals that are hunted by other animals for food
SERRATIONS	small notches or teeth like a saw that help to cut
TROPICAL	hot and humid
UNIQUE	being the only one of its kind

INDEX